LOVECATION

A TRUE LOVE IN VERSE

YAHAYA BALOGUN

authorHOUSE

AuthorHouse™
1663 Liberty Drive
Bloomington, IN 47403
www.authorhouse.com
Phone: 833-262-8899

Published by AuthorHouse 07/09/2021

ISBN: 978-1-6655-3126-9 (sc)
ISBN: 978-1-6655-3127-6 (hc)
ISBN: 978-1-6655-3130-6 (e)

Library of Congress Control Number: 2021913710

Contents

Introduction

"Love is a smoke made with the fume of sighs"
- Act 1, Scene 1, Lines 197-198 in Shakespeare's Romeo and Juliet

"I had no time to HATE because
The Grave would hinder me,
And life was not so ample
I could FINISH the enmity.

Nor had I time to LOVE, but since
Some industry must be,
The little toil of love, I THOUGHT,
Was large enough for me."

- Emily Dickinson

Preface

Poetry as a genre of Literature is an area to which not many literary buffs love to venture because of peculiarities associated with it. Unlike prose, poetry adds artistic style to writing in an elevated language, howbeit with the economical use of words. Poetry expresses more profound feelings in communication than other genres because of vivid imageries and rhythms. It's this reason that William Wordsworth, the 18th-century poet of nature, famously posited that "Poetry is a spontaneous overflow of powerful feelings." This is not farther than the truth.

The purgation of feelings is more poignant if it is a love poem. It's in this connection that Yahaya Balogun's collection of poetry is a book that takes the readers on a long voyage in the vast ocean of life where romantic love is portrayed as an elixir to arouse deep feelings. This collection is a book whose primary theme is love and how two love birds can serenade each other, add more flavor, and garnish their love life with the flowery words coated in honeyed rhythms.

The author, Yahaya Balogun, a prolific writer himself who knows his literary onion and peels it with great skill and dexterity, doesn't disappoint the readers by adroitly deploying it scintillating words put his thoughts across. All the poems in the collection are blank verses, which means the poet doesn't follow the traditional or formalistic style of rhyming schemes. The readers lose rhyming; the poet generously deploys them in imageries, figures, and other devices that make them crave to read the poems with delight and gusto.

This collection of poems is a book that should enrich every family's bookshelf and individuals who are desirous of keeping the flame of their

love burning. According to the poet: Love is inexpensive to give as a gift. Gift of Love is expansive to haters. Wrap love as a bundle of gifts to resenters." These lines are pungent and instructive to all and sundry who desire to bring great joy to their lives even if they are not that rich materially; they should be rich at heart through thick and thin. That's the central theme of the poems in this collection.

The author, therefore, should be commended for adding to the growing list of the anthology of poems. It will spark the zeal of the readers in embracing poetry as a genre of Literature. On the one hand and the other hand, this will turn their world into heaven through powerful and moving romantic words that fill them with pleasure and illuminate their lives.

Barrister Abdullah Korede, Lagos, Nigeria.
May 31, 2021

Acknowledgments

The idea of this work was conceived a few months ago as I mused about various developments in the world. War and peace struggle with each other, and while peace eludes the globe, war reigns supreme in the heart of the leaders in our troubled world. Love starts from every family with multiplier effects. In every family and satisfying relationship resides love and different recipes to prepare the naughtiness of unconditional and true love.

I appreciate my lovely family for their patience and unconditional love. My family's patience and understanding afforded me the opportunity and time to write at all times. My heartfelt appreciation also goes to those committed colleagues, friends, and esteemed followers on social and electronic media. They are parts of the sources of inspiration for writing the manuscript that morphed into this book. My admirers' names are too numerous to mention, but they all know themselves after reading this token of appreciation. We must always find time to treat ourselves to "lovecation" and true love to bring amity to the world.

Dedication

This book is dedicated to lovebirds in genuine relationships.

Your Smile Takes Me Away

Take candy away from me!
If you wish, take muteness away,
But do not take from me the smile
Of my Muse and soulmate.

Do not take away the care,
The tenderness heart that you make;
That soothes my being.
The joy of your presence,
That suddenly moved to another space.

Tears not forth in our happiness,
The sudden wave of change born in you,
Is suitable for your advancement.
The divine designer means well for you.
Leverage it!

Initially, my struggle to cope
With your absence, tore
My teary eyes and soul.
I miss your closeness and vibes.

Now, your daily presence in my heart
Recompense your abrupt presence.
I muse your beautiful smile
As a therapeutic wave to my excited soul.
Your presence in my heart renews my joy!

Your Smile
Takes Me
Away

Handzyprints

My Precious Gemstone

The poppet one was naked,
And deliberately my choice.
She is nestled in her inviting wrapper,
And her orotund voice charms
The mind of a willing man.
She is not only amorous but curled
In her moment of glory.

A world of glittering jewel
And precious stones,
Dazzling with a quick rhythm
Of love in mind.
Her gait stunningly ravishing
The pace of her opposite.
The speed of lights and sounds
In her voice is refreshing.

Alluringly uncovered,
She becomes my praises,
Smiling from the depth
Of the beauty on her couch.
At the invitation of her look,
I trekked with triumph
And "Pride of Barbados" to answer
Her alluring call of nature.

As I made the eagerly move
To lure her, I observed her rotund head.
Her English head is tangled with blond hair.

Her body supports the glossy smooth
Of her doubled twinkling buttock anchored
In her elaborated hips.

Her right and her arms are undulating
In the thin air as a quill.
Her beauty lured my want-to-do
In ambulatory plan towards her armory.
In her pubic asset resides the joy
Of our eternal ecstasy!

My Precious
GEMSTONE

A Loving Night at the Love Zone

After a day of unrest!
We retired quietly in our rows.
Each of us is nestled in our space
I was contemplating the following action.
To sleep or not to sleep, or to copulate!
But who will make the first move?

The bright light in our room dissolved
Into darkness and color of love.
I extended my integral part lusciously!
A tingling sensation kinked my earlobes.
I whispered to her accessible ear
With romantic and sentimental emotions.
Who will make the first move?

The loud silence in the room melted
To prepare a wailing soul ready for coupling.
The agitation on our sides is noticeable
As the sumptuous souls are readily apparent.
But who will make the first move?

As I lovingly sauntered horizontally,
She ambled obliquely to meet
A man who was mutually in need of her soul.
In an instant, two minds morphed into an ecstatic zone.
Into a natural action that defined the night.
Bodies are burrowed in the ecstasy of love.
The rest of the night was recounted in ecstasy.

A Loving Night
at the
Love Zone

The Winter is Here

All night long in summer,
He groans under the tutelage of heat!
Summer isn't an impediment to lovemaking.
It only creates an aura of uneasiness.
Now, winter is here; they're deliciously ready.

All night long in summer,
He mesmerizes her with climate change
In their moist and sensual room.
Summer isn't a clog in their fondness.
It only makes the atmosphere
Of lovemaking quick and easy.
Now, winter is here; they're mutually beneficial.

All night long in summer,
She feels unburdened but bordered
With the darkness but not the room climate.
Summer is climatic for nurtured love.
It only gives buffers to the expectations
Of the winter wrapped up in mutual love.

THE WINTER IS HERE

A Shinning Star On The Hill

She is a worshipper of the Muse.
Her mien is lured with confidence!
Her inviting smiley outlook is flavorful.
Whereas confidence is sexy!
Her confidence neutralizes our timidity!

She combines the rare qualities of a gem:
Brilliance, beauty inwards, and outwards endowment.
Call her Amazon; I call her a Muse and Icon.
An icon of inspiration and love.
I call her Mama Nnedinso; they call her enthusiast!

Last night, I dwelt in a literary cocoon
I busted out of silent laughter!
I didn't realize my state of sanity
Until names like Nnedinso Ogaziechi
Chimamanda Ngozi, W.S Soyinka,
Chinua Achebe and other literati flooded
My insatiable literary mind.

She has been an impetus of new love.
She gives love, and she receives grace and love.
You never know how beautiful you are
Until you see the colony of admirers streaming
Your real life of humanity.
She's our Muse; celebrate her with your fecundity!

A SHINING STAR
on the HILL

A Red Letter Day For Our Literary Muse

Clinging to a glass of wine
In absentia of her Muse.
She is a brilliant literatus!
She floats in the euphoria
Of love and care!
A great Mother with Mother care!
Her poise, brilliance, and elegance
Is mused and loved always!
She celebrates others
Like she celebrates her own.

She is our unique icon!
An icon of inspiration to all.
Her birthday is an "August" Day!
An "August" occasion worthy
Of wine and dine!!
The poignancy of her mind;
The expression of her Muse
In others is much rated with love!

In a red-letter and unique Days
Like Mama Nnedinso's,
You're pregnant with her literary
Ace and sharp mind.
On her day, you are studded
With uncountable literary words.

Yet! She deserves stainless words
On her red-letter day!

This woman deserves
The celebration of her fecund mind.
And she cares for humanity!
Her love for humanity knows no bounds!

**A Red Letter Day
For Our
LITERARY MUSE**

The Gift of Love

Love is inexpensive to give as a gift.
Gift of Love is expansive to haters
Wrap love as a bundle of gifts to resenters
Don't tremble under their tutelage of hate.
Give love as a gift to replace hate.

Never quiver the hearts that hate.
Instead, give them love to situate affection
In their hearts of hatred and misery.
Feed the hearts that wander around
To enjoy the new and warm love.

Love is a perfume fuming in amity
Share love, give love to needy of love
In the hearts of haters is hidden love.
Unearthing love in them will blossom lives.
Give love to haters to feel being loved.

The gift of love is a gift of life.
Give a bundle of gifts for love to flourish
Flourishing love brings peace and unity.
Love cannot be bought but can be freely
Offered to ailing hearts in need of love.

The Gift
of Love

The Stolen Heart

In a tranquilized night of love
I sliced through its darkness,
What I see is the bubbling heart
Anxiously pumping the blood of love.

She laid down in expectation of ecstasy.
I prowled and crawled with cling in lust
As I rhythmically cleared my throat
She corralled my inviting look to tame her.

She sauntered in her trunk to welcome
My essence of love ensconced in a row.
A night of celebration of mutual love.
Love entangled in endless minutes of five
We both dissolved in the dark of dusk.
I recovered my stolen heart at dawn.

The Stolen
Heart

A Date With Myself

Every sunset is an
Opportunity to muse my day.
Every dusk is a chance
To take stock of my actions and inactions.
I muse my failures and successes
To prepare for a new day.
I dwell daily in self-love
And self-validation!

At dawn,
I wake up refreshed.
I invoke the Most Excellency
To start a new day.
I pay close attention to my environment.
Life is beautiful if your heart's
Insignia is love and grace.

Each day, I am faced
Between what is right
And what is expedient.
I chose the former; I jettisoned the latter!
Each day is another opportunity
To correct the blunders of yesterday.

The good I do today is a catalyst
To leverage my joy for tomorrow.
When tomorrow seems farfetched,
I use today's normalcy
Through mindfulness to face

Probably tomorrow.
Because tomorrow isn't too far
But full of uncertainties and possibilities!
I am who I am; I love myself!
Call it self-love:
I call it a ceaseless date with myself!
I am normal in an abnormal society!
Being normal is a literal enzyme
That gives me internal joy.
You never know how awesome
You are by loving and being yourself;
Being loved and beloved!
I give myself a date!
Life is concise!
Enjoy every moment while it lasts!

A DATE WITH MYSELF

My Holy Crime Of Love

I want to commit a crime Of love
At the basement of your holy dome!
I want to serve my time
In the prison of your molybdic.
Who'll be the judge to pronounce
My sentence?

Your crafted body will preside
Over my infatuation.
In the court of love, I will keep silent
To get subsumed in the pronouncement
Of my guilt of love for you as charged.

I will romanticize my love offense,
And submit for the incarceration of love.
I will plead guilty to have my pen
In your point-institution forever!
Your endowed holy mountain will be my coagulated cell.

A concentration camp of love
To unleash our affections,
And to savor my lovely and holy crime.
I want you as my partner in a crime of love.
If I don't commit myself, I will be a free man
For not confessing my love.

My freedom in the worldly affairs
Will be nonplussed.
I am lovingly guilty as charged
By my terrific love for you in the prison of love

My Holy Crime Of Love

Handzyprints

The Dancing Beauty

The stage was perfumed with sensual lights.
I gleamed my expectant eyes, bemusing her.
The figure-eight in her mien glazed my heart.
I sauntered to the front stage to feed
My sensual appetite and lusciousness in her.

The crowd was unaware of my sinister gestures,
Intentions and mind mission.
As my mind was completely wrapped in ecstasy,
She walked the stage with alluring confidence
In sexuality and candor.

The more I stared at her, the more
Her sensuous part dazed my vision.
She is a winsome angel; she's a bewitching
Pearl mesmerizing the sacred part of me.
I feel lucky to have her as a gaiety partner.

The dance of love is entwined in her glory.
As the crowd applauded her mesmerizing
Display on stage, my mind took a French leave
To cherish the aura of love, she ensued.
As she descended the stage,
I flinched our departure to my expectant
Imagination of fingering and sexual night.

The Dancing
Beauty

Handzyprints

Longer Than A Platonic Year

A platonic year was far longer than expected.
One month I lived without you was unending.
The thought of you overwhelms my breath
The degree of my recall
Of you daunted.

But again, seeing your beautiful face
Did not faze my affection for you.
Your absence deconstructed the myth
Of love, while you are way in a
mindful distance.

Let us embark on a journey we long
To see in our mutual love and affection.
In a jiffy, your journey seems far!
But the chemistry is shared.

While in the towering of love,
Your showering of affection is mused
In the platonic ocean of your tenderness.
I long for your coming home soon
Where our collective fondness
Will be cherished again.

LONGER THAN A
PLATONIC YEAR

Hug me tight for amity

I am a hugger with courteous attention.
Every sight of me to you is blessed with attention.
I crave genuine affection and love with attention.
Of the affection-receiver; and affection-donor.

Hugging is soothing and therapeutic.
It brings the beneficiary of huggers to amity.
Hugging validates the esteem of players.
Please give me one hug,
And I will provide you with many hugs in return.

Unconsciously, I give hugs with ease!
Sometimes, I get cold shoulders and shrugs.
But the authenticity in me gives way for satisfaction.
Tight hugs can be a great gift.
To those in need of succor and peace.

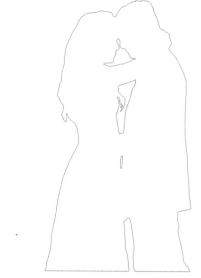

HUG ME TIGHT FOR AMITY

The Wintry Winter

Her abode is windy and cold!
The winter is wintry in cloudy clime.
On top of her house is snuggery to keep her cozy.
Winter is here; the best time of the year.

I wish I can be in a snuggery mode
In the comfort zone of a house in peace!
It is not impossible to have one for Muse.
The possibility depends on mutual desires.

Do not lose the hope of cuddling!
Muse, the presence of your partner.
The feelings are mutual, but one is a spook.
The other is carefully thought and care.

Give assurance in mutuality to tame secrets.
The mind will reset for reassurance!
Don't give other supporters your secrets.
Your supporters have other supporters,
Who will tell your secrets to others
As the winter blows the wind of love.
Let's dissolve into the sensual night.

THE WINTRY WINTER

Her Footsteps lured me

Love, something crazy comes to mind:
I can't bear living on my best behavior."
– Louise Label

I am ensconced on my homely couch
Bit by bit, she ecstatically sauntered towards me:
In advance of my expectant body
She moved in a quiet gusto to ease my luscious appetite....

Beautiful being, purely-shaped in elegance---
Her pace was intentional; how sugar-candied!
Gosh!--every knack of her I have imagined
Comes to my naked mind from those bare feet.
Her inviting mien lured my readied hull
to be criminal of love in her prison.

Her riveting beauty is a rarity in reality;
Only I can express it in a closed encounter
As my mind traveled a million miles
To capture her essence,
My trembling heart aced and imagined
The expected and indescribable action.
Oh! I waste no time with a luring heart
Waiting to be swilled in the cup of love.

HER FOOTSTEPS LURED ME

On Your Wedding Day

Your days are numbered:
On your wedding day,
You'll be in the smitten-nest of your suitor
A Day you will be incommunicado and cagey.
Some call weddings a road to the prison of love;
Some allude to it as conjugal marriage.

On your wedding day,
You'll dance in the full glare of the crowds
To the celebration of your own defeat.
Your woman and nature will nurture your libido
Your beautiful beauty will tame you
With her smitten-nest.

On your wedding day,
You'll lose your freedom anew for life and death.
The D-day ahead is not meant for every man.
Only the dedicated men have affirmed the victims
In your impending prison of love.

On your wedding day,
The married men in attendance will empathize
With your incognizance and naivety as you help
Your suitor to prepare your endless smitten-nest.
Where the ‹rumpy-pumpy' and topsy-turvy will meet
To celebrate your future rout and defeat.

On Your
Wedding Day

Our Entwined Love in Absentia.

When I look through your eyes,
What I see is pure love and care.
In absentia, my mind entwines your mind.
Knowing you is happiness,
Loving you is a dream fulfilled and mused.

As night and day interchange,
I long to kiss you a thousand times!
I see the blooming lips and jim-dandy
Reciprocating my craves for your presence.
How long will I have to wait to kiss you?

Can I talk about your motivational acuity?
Or your sensual look combined with intelligence
Love is a smoke made with the fume of a sigh.
As I look at you, you look at me, alas!
It is so clear that you know how I feel.
I call it to love; you name it, sound vibration.

The Day I will meet you will be August day.
A day the true minds will meet to show
Mutual eternal love and affection.
I feel our pure love.
I have discerned our conjoined fondness.
It's called unhurt, spotless, and puppy love.

OUR ENTWINED
LOVE IN ABSENTIA

The Flame of Love

The heat of love
Storms my stomach with many expectations.
As I scurry through a rail of emotions to feel you,
I stumble on affection burning with flames of love.
The more I try to control the feeling I have for you,
My mind is arrested with the laden of emotions.
I see my longings in the cubicle of your heart.

The flame of love
Cannot be quenched with levity and loathe.
"Love is a smoke made with (serious) fume of sigh."
As time ticks in the ticktock of time, love is slicked.
The feeling is indescribably soothing and wowed.
I dwell in amity and a fond gulf of love.

The ashes of love bubbles
In the durable and flammable clime.
The clime is being consumed in the cloud of love
I get entangled in the angst and intensity of love,
As I feel the connection of emotions in a bloom,
My mind is unfolding in the freshness of intimacy.
Let's cling tonight in the kinky duvet of love.

THE FLAME OF LOVE

Her Love is Amity

I crave affection; she gives me love.
Her gentle feeling of caring gives me amity.
I seek to get attention; she bestows me comfort.
Her spotlight in my heart heralds optimism.
A life of love is a life to live.

I love her personality; she enjoys everything.
Her beauty represents her attitude.
She gives care effortlessly to the lineage of love.
She is a beauty to behold.
She's an adorable gift of love.
A life of love embellishes the beauty in her.

HER LOVE IS AMITY

In Our Absence

Barely a few days,
We have scarcely departed
When your charming image
Crystalline my thoughts.
Can you wait for me? I am ensconced
In a folder of your Muse.

My dearest love,
We have found each other in the enclave
Of smitten love with your irresistible image.
Our bodies are thirsty for shared love.
Our mouths are dripping.
For wine, clinging, and kisses.

Let me meet you at the love zone
To smitt my craving love for you.
I am so hungry for you in your absence.
Please wait for me to catch up with you
Your absence burns like a furnace flame.
Come back to me.

IN OUR ABSENCE

Wind of Love On the Island

The wind of love.
It is blowing in perpetuity of ecstasy.
Is your wind a horse or donkey?
He runs through my wild mind to take me
Far away from your come-hitter zone.
I am ready for the hurricane of love.

Let me indulge and dance
In the theater of your enticing soul,
Please don't make me a gale spectator on stage
As we dance to the celebration of our fusion.
Let the stormy wind not be a burden to us;
Let the wind of love encircle us.

While we dwell in the wind of love,
Let us not listen to the howling of the wind.
With your brow eyes on my forehead,
I see your luring mouth on my waiting lips
Ready to gaggle your wetted mouth
In the windy winter of love.

WIND OF LOVE ON THE ISLAND

In The Love Zone

All night long,
I have slept in your inviting zone.
I dreamt of the sea of love by the river bank.
You were wild; I was untamed within your thigh,
With fire and unexplainable pleasure, I sunk in
The red precinct of your alluring enclave.

In the love zone,
I saw through your tempting eyes.
Perhaps belatedly, our dreams conjoined
At the imaginary sixty-nine clime of ecstasy.
Up above was the split of moves by our habitual noise.
We clung weirdly in the regional climate of love.

In the deep blue sea,
I strolled in my dreams,
Even without sighting you, I heap upon you.
I sailed in you like a merriment voyagers
Served with the tasteful sandwich, wine, and love---
You are the anchor to the gifts of my love life.

IN THE LOVE ZONE

Handzyprints

I Love Her Like A Goddess

She's a muse and sweetness of heart.
Her smiles enliven the beauty of fascinating creatures.
Beneath the layout of her mind is raw intellect.
Give her an assignment, she executes it diligently
With brilliance, it requires.

She's a blunt shooter with integrity.
Her disposition to facts is mused and adored.
Every step she takes is gracefully noticed.
She holds no grudges nor detests anyone.
But her zero tolerance for idiocy is absolute.

Good and fertile hearts love her.
Her identity is her honest representation.
Everywhere she goes, she radiates confidence.
Her steady composure gives others stability.
Every hug she bestows tranquilizes souls.

She's destined to change lives.
Her scion is lucky to have her as a momma.
She's everything to her siblings.
Her wisdom to tame difficult situations is raw.
She's loved; she's mused; she's respected.
She's everything adorable to the wise ones around.

I LOVE HER LIKE
A GODDESS

I Muse Her Presence

Her image is light; it illuminates dark hearts.
She's a sweet bird, enthralling the murky minds.
The mind is a beautiful thing to behold.
She never loses her sterling focus on morality.
Every step she takes gives direction to love life.
Her wayfaring assists a wandering mind.

Give me her portrait of love and affection.
I will archive her pictures in my album of love
My devotion to love her is unblemished.
I care to see her a thousand times a day.
The more you remember her alluring
Heart, the more you're enthralled by her gait.

Her presence conveniently roommates us.
We are livable in the comfort of her siren heart.
She has no pretense for loony behavior.
The heart that tells lies is a danger to everyone.
Get me your soul to mimic for my life essence,
Let your remedial presence bear the witness
To Souls in the race of life for amity.

I MUSE HER PRESENCE

Far Longer Than A Platonic Year

A platonic year was far
Longer than expected.
One month I lived without you
Was unending.
The thought of you overwhelms
My breadth.
The degree of my recall of you daunted.

But again,
Seeing your beautiful face
Did not Faze my affection for you.
Your absence deconstructed the myth of love.

**FAR LONGER THAN A
PLATONIC YEAR**

Handzyprints

The Sanctuary of Love

She made her
Pilgrimage to the man's haven.
What happened in that sanctuary of a man.
It is only known to temptress and the twosome!
She is endowed with God's gifts and men's nemesis.
Onlookers at the love vineyard are guilty
Of prurient viewing of upper and Lower Extremities.
Lookers aren't excluded from her fortified traps.

The daughter of a man
Elopes on a mission of
Holy moly to slay the soul of a fragile mind.
A man's mind is always pregnant with (in)fidelity.
Only the strong minds in the luscious climes
Of the daughter of Eve can survive the temptation.
From the cradle, man is nurtured by the milk
Of woman; nature to commit tryst and twirled leisure.

Sensual women baits
The son of a man's mind.
No man is immune to her decoys and nestles.
Her smitten-nest is a burden to careless souls.
The immortality of man makes him susceptible
To hanky-panky and baits of the daughter of Eve.
The mind of a man is wired to fall prey to her prowling.
A man ever stands sheepish to her "tasty" invites.

Her mission is not
Unknown to the son of Adam.
When the mission is mutually accomplished
In love's sanctuary, the scandal is opened.
And imminently unmuted by the children of cyborgs.
The zuckerville will soon avail the cooking affair.
Nattering ants on cyberspace will relish in a liaison
Between the consensual adults in jiggery-pokery.

THE SANCTUARY OF LOVE

Feed The Minds Of Hate with Love

They have wretched minds with false beliefs.
Inside of them is robust instruments of hate!
They have no qualms for the right things
Ironically, most of them come from the far-right
With the whirlwind minds of evils and misdeeds
They see sins as excellent and good as evils.
A man's mind is wasted in the cocoon of evil

Conspiracy theorists are human beings
Warped in mind to thread the path of self-destruct
They have no clue of what is missing from them
When you see them, you will recognize them
They are destroyers of decent image.
Seditious minds force the end to be a beginning.
Their beginnings always equate ends.

They believe in aliens invasion of the Earth
Lies and unbelievable things are natural to them
Fringe-believers are a menace to themselves
And the existential threat to selves and society
They are at the edge of their group mindset.
Conspiracy theorists have altered ego and cognition
The more you love fringe elements, the more
They swim in the ocean of hate and resentment.
Give them Love to feed the hunger of hate.

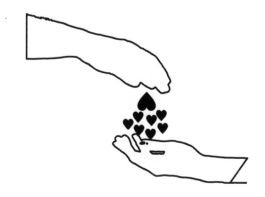

FEED THE MINDS OF
HATE WITH LOVE

Women: The Smitten Idols of Humanity

We were first aliens in mother's smitten-nests.
We were illegal immigrants to women's tubes.
Tera (trillions) of us escaped from the beleaguered world of men
Through the climax. It was the first survival
Of the fittest during coitus to safety.

As we swim across the ocean of solitude,
The strong trample upon the weak
To berge-in women's wombs.
Women allow their maternal weapons
As roads, through which we travel,
To seek refuge from man's pungent release.

Women defy all odds; they brook the political rants.
They fight and struggle with maternal weapons.
And take us as maternal refugees.
Men are terrors in schism, with much audacity to inflict anguish.
Men are enfant terrible in their nocuous cocoons.
Men are scamps.

Women are clement Idols. They are forbearers,
And messengers of peace and endurance to humanity.
Salutation and love to our women.

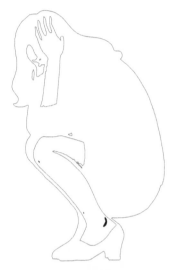

WOMEN:
THE SMITTEN IDOLS
OF HUMANITY

I Want To Be A Flower

In my next world,
I want to reincarnate as a flower.
My choice of empyreal lair will be Amsterdam;
A charming city in Holland.
I will either be a flower to a king,
Or a king to a queen of flowers.
Flowers embellish their host (tree and land);
They give hope and love to hopelessness.
Flowers depict peace;
A tranquilizer to troubled minds.
When a man receives flowers,
It bequeaths his soul with beauty.
It transmutes the giver's mind
To love.
When a man gives flowers,
It tranquilizes the receiver's mind to amity.
At birth, the soul is welcomed to live with flowers.
In death, the soul departs life with flowers.
A flower is a love. A flower is a life.
In my reincarnation,
In a world of intense existential angst to relieve souls,
I want to be a flower.

I WANT TO BE A
Flower

Our Chemistry, Our Hearts

We live on magic Island and sanctuary
Where love is bonded in multiple folds.
To some, love is indescribable; to us
Love is indestructible but tough and enduring!
We're dwellers in love vineyards.

We have had a roller coaster of love.
Now, it's time to taste the scent of passion
Mixed with ingredients and sauces of love.
I crave the expanse of our mutual love
And the expectation of clinging every night.

Love is a wine made with the scent of passion.
The more we glimpse at the mystery of love
The more we celebrate the unending bond
In our mutual mystery of affection and favor.
Love is kind and sweet to seamless souls
Who are in an unblemished
Agreement of love?

A Kiss Of Life

Her wetted lips are very inviting!
High stake in the sweetened and expected night.
She melted my heart with sturdy, attractive eyes.
Love is beautiful, and beauty is passion-making.
I unmasked my hidden and eager lips to kiss
Her moistened mouth was brimming
with an invite.

The twilight day melted into a glowing night.
I sauntered with readiness to plant the edges
Of my longing lips to taste the kiss of life.
She surrendered to my willing soul to tame her.
Kiss me, kiss me, babe, on a magical night
Prepped with spices of love.

While I professed my love
in the day and nightfall, She redefined
The definition of love and care.
Sweet love, sweethearts, and soulmate
Mingling and mining the treasures of love.
Passionate bussing of her is healing
To a wandering soul
In search of love.

A Kiss Of *Life*

Love At First Sight

The sun shines in a coaching arcade.
The sanctuary of love opened in your heart.
We emit the emotional tenderness
And the warmth of our love life.
Let the secrets of love flourish in our hearts.
Let us uncovered to the world our fondness.

The sight of you triggered a strange gaze.
Call it lust. I call it garnishment of love.
The blooming and fresh air refreshed us
To appreciate the beauty of love.
I craved your love. They desire their lust for you.
Lust and love are mutually exclusive.

The rubicund in our souls desire each other.
While we look tamed in the treaty of love,
Your onlookers lust for your sumptuous beauty.
In your glamour and moral compass,
They're mesmerized by the inherent beauty
You ensued and glossed over.

Love At First Sight

In The Twilight Of The Night.

The sun dissolved into the twilight day.
The bird perched on the surface of its nest.
My soul dreamed of the splendid night.
I gazed at her inviting image with a luring look.
I visualized the unanimous night with her
Alluring beauty.

It was a perfect night.
In a night that imagined the dawn of time.
She ambulated her beauty with gaiety steps
Our dusk bloomed with promising days ahead.
Loving her is loving life of love.

Before we agree to part with a beautiful morning,
My heart was skipping the rope of love
You are the flower that blooms my heart.
The sparkling water in your eyes buds the
Rolling water in my eyes--I am tamed by your
Alluring gaze at my receptive soul waiting
To receive your beautiful souls.

In The Twilight
Of The Night

Let There Be Love!

Let there
Be love and lovers.
Love is not alien. Love is love.
Love knows no boundaries!
"Love is smoke made with the fume
of sigh." Do not impede love.

Let there
Be love and lovers in your
Cafe. Give lovers the platform to flourish
And nourish the ecstasy of affection.
Be the cord of love to connect impending
Lovers. The lovers of love must cling in your
Abode. Funke cannot halt
Impending lovers.

True love
Cannot be destroyed.
Love brings concord and cordiality.
Cordiality brings amity. Amity brings harmony.
Harmony engenders peace for the world.
Funke, bring the twosome back to grease
And make love in your
Zucker sanctuary.

Let There Be Love

Let's Nestle In A Quiet Place.

Keep away your devices.
Let's ambulate to a quiet place to dine.
Keep away all existential distractions.
Make us a friendly betrothed and lovebirds.
Let's exhibit mutual love and banish
Ourselves into the etching and sleeping
Beauty to quietly make love.

Keep away your devices.
Drop your gadgets and pads in the
Closet. Let's have a dead silence in a recluse
Place. To rehearse love and create devotion
To us. Let's prepare mutual amity to play love.
The beach is howling for our "lovecation.'
Make our tabernacles provide ecstasy
Under the shades of love.

Keep away your devices.
Let's banish ourselves in the tingling
Noises of lust. Give me fertile ground for
Passion and vigor. Let's nestle in the
Small nest. Where breeze preps our souls,
And the sounds of choir birds singing
To excite and nestle
Our willing souls.

Let's Nestle In A
Quiet Place

Comments About the Book

"The Poems bridge the gap between life and music. The magnanimity of its therapeutical nature reflects in the manner by which it appeals to mind, soul, and heart. The dexterity and how the author weaves and coins words to communicate his thoughts across is in this magnanimous medium. It also reflects the ingenuity of his choice of words and theme in writing. The central theme, love, speaks spectacularly to the complexity of human relations and communication. The author is known for his riveting style of writing and musing, which originally stands him out as an impeccably established writer of note. This collection of poems will no doubt be a boon to lovers to add more fillip to their relationship further."

- Funke Cole is a doctoral candidate in History at the prestigious University of Lagos, Lagos, Nigeria (2021).

From Politics To Lovecation

Humans love, and humans play politics. Without love, there will be no politics because politics is a by-product of love relationships, good or bad, short or long-lasting.

The writer, Yahaya Balogun, has delved into a familiar topic, away from the norm, regarding his writing style and focus. He has delved into politics and its nuances that produce bad, excellent, or fair leaderships across the globe but more especially in his native country Nigeria and adopted country, the United States of America.

Politics comes with the familiar divisiveness and the famed permanent interests, power, and attendant influences. Yahaya Balogun, therefore, tried to poetically explore the powerful uniting force of the universal phenomenon of Love and Lovemaking. To him, nothing on Earth has the power that comes with the feeling of loving and being loved. No race, gender, class, politics, or creed interferes when genuine consensual love is in view.

The genre through which love is best expressed is poetry, and the author effectively deploys this literary medium to pass the universal message of love, loving, sensuality, and lovemaking.

The language of love, the universality of its nuances, comes off to the author as uniquely human without any doubt. He aptly uses his poetic license all through the collection. He tags his foray with this writing style from politics to love, sensuality that undoubtedly leads to lovemaking with a global uniformity in style and content, LOVECATION.

Hilarious but factual, his foray into semantic ingenuity is exhilaratingly honest and as bluntly authentic as he could paint with words and sharp, unambiguous imageries. His use of imageries and various figures of speech shows his literary fecundity.

A collection of poems dedicated to lovebirds in genuine relationships come as a true elixir to a world on the edge of the precipice with conflicts coming off the backs of politics and religion. These two human experiences ought with love be uniting forces rather than the divisive factors in our world.

The collection starts with a piece on SMILE...the first visual invitation to any love relationship. This powerful imagery from the author shows he fully understands the human instincts and the ingredients of love and lovemaking. A Smile is priceless and calming and a precursor to any relationship, more so a consensual one between lovers. Then he goes ahead to use the most appropriate register to stir, amuse and entertain his readers.

Does Yahaya achieve his aim of 'distracting' from the tension of politics to the allure of love and loving? Absolutely! A picture well painted without any exaggerated sense of puritanism. The language is bare of any hypocrisies, which points to the author's genuineness and importance of accuracy. A poetic rendition that is as engaging as it is entertaining and calming. I recommend this collection.

Nnedinso Ogaziechi, Lagos, Nigeria.
May 30, 2021

Lightning Source UK Ltd.
Milton Keynes UK
UKHW011836190721
387436UK00001B/31